good answers
to tough questions

About Change and Moving

Written by Joy Berry

 CHILDRENS PRESS ®

CHICAGO

Managing Editor: Lana Eberhard

Copy Editors: Annette Gooch, Judy Lockwood

Contributing Editors: Margie Austin, John Bilitch, Ph.D.,
Libby Byers, Ilene Frommer, James Gough, M.D.,
Dan Gurney, Charles Pengra, Ph.D.

Art Direction: Communication Graphics

Designer: Jennifer Wiezel

Illustration Designer: Bartholomew

Inking Artist: Berenice Happe Iriks

Lettering Artist: Linda Hanney

Coloring Artist: Christine McNamara

Typography and Production: Communication Graphics

Published by Childrens Press
in cooperation with Living Skills Press

This book can answer the following questions:
- What changes happen in you?
- What changes happen in your situation?
- What are unwanted changes?
- How can you adapt to unwanted change?
- How can you adapt to moving?

When something changes, it becomes different. It is no longer the way it was. Nothing ever stays exactly the same. Everything changes in one way or another.

Like everything else, you too are changing. You are becoming different in one way or another every moment you live. You are never exactly the same as you were.

Your **body** is always changing.

There are continual changes in the **size** of your body.

WOW. LAST YEAR THIS JACKET FIT ME PERFECTLY. THIS YEAR IT'S **TOO** SMALL. THE SIZE OF MY BODY KEEPS CHANGING.

There are also continual changes in the **shape** of your body.

There are continual changes in the **appearance** of your body. Usually this happens so slowly that you might not notice much change in your appearance over a short time. But from year to year, you can see a big change.

There are also continual changes in the **functioning** of your body (the way it works).

In addition to your body, your **knowledge** (what you know) is always changing.

Your *personality* is also constantly changing.

Just as you are always changing, your *situation* (the people, places, things, and experiences in your life) is always changing.

There are continual changes in the people who are part of your life.

There are also changes in the **places** where you live, play, go to school, and do other things.

There are changes in the kinds of **things** you have and use.

There are also changes in the kinds of **experiences** you have (the things you do and the things that happen around you).

Sometimes you might welcome a particular change in your situation. Other times you might not.

Unwelcome changes are called **unwanted changes.** There are several kinds of unwanted changes.

Sometimes you might be afraid that a particular change will hurt you in some way. This is called a **threatening change**.

Sometimes another person or situation might force you to make a change you have not chosen for yourself. This is called an **imposed change**.

Sometimes you might dislike a particular change so much that accepting it seems impossible. This is called an **unacceptable change**.

Sometimes a change might happen suddenly without your knowing that it is going to occur. This is called an **unexpected change.**

Sometimes there is no way to tell how a particular change will turn out. This is called an **unpredictable change**.

Unwanted changes can cause you to feel uncomfortable. They can also be difficult to handle. You might wish you could avoid unwanted changes.

Although you can have control over many of the changes in your life, it is impossible for you to have complete control over all of them. This is especially true of unwanted changes. *Unwanted changes are a natural part of every human being's life.*

Since it is impossible for you to avoid all unwanted changes, it is important for you to learn to handle them appropriately. When you handle a change appropriately, it has a positive effect on your life.

There are six steps to handling unwanted change appropriately:

Step One: Face it.
Step Two: Accept it.
Step Three: Learn all you can about it.
Step Four: Decide what you can do about it.
Step Five: Follow through with your decisions.
Step Six: Continue to talk about the change until you have adapted to it.

When you **adapt** to a change, you get used to it. You adjust to it. When you adapt to a change, you no longer focus on it in a way that interferes with the rest of your life.

Adapting usually happens so gradually that you might not notice it is happening.

Sometimes moving (going to live someplace else) can be
- a threatening change,
- an imposed change,
- an unacceptable change,
- an unexpected change, or
- an unpredictable change.

This is why children often consider moving to be an unwanted change.

Moving can cause children to feel
- insecure because they do not know what is going to happen to them in the new location
- worried that they won't like living in their new home,
- sad at having to leave the people and places that are familiar to them,
- frustrated because they feel as if they cannot control what is happening to them, and
- overwhelmed because they have to start over, make new friends, and develop a new life for themselves.

Moving can cause children to think these kinds of thoughts:
- Why don't I get to decide whether I will stay or move? It's not fair that other people can make this decision for me!
- Will I ever see my friends again? What will I do without them? What if I don't make any new friends?
- I feel comfortable and secure in this house and neighborhood because I know them so well. How will I learn everything I need to know about the new house and neighborhood?
- What if I don't like the new neighborhood and the new school?
- What is going to happen to me?

Someday it might be necessary for you to move. If this should happen, there are things you can do to help yourself adapt to the change. Follow these six steps:

Step One: Face it.

Face the fact that the change is taking place.

Step Two: Accept it.

Give in to the reality that you will be moving. Do not resist it. Fighting the change will only make things harder for yourself and the people around you.

Step Three: Learn all you can about it.

When you do not have enough factual information about something, your mind often makes up its own thoughts about it. Sometimes these thoughts are frightening. Even though the thoughts might not be true, they can cause you to feel uncomfortable.

It is important to find out all the information you can about your future move. Try to find out
- why you have to move,
- where you will be moving, and
- when you will be moving.

Also, learn all you can about
- your new home and the new neighborhood,
- the school you will attend,
- the church, temple, or synagogue you might attend,
- parks and other areas where you can play, and
- community programs and activities available to people your age.

You can learn the information you need to know by visiting your new home and the new community.

You can also learn the information you need to know by
- talking or writing to the real estate or rental agent who helps your parents find a new home for your family,
- introducing yourself to your new neighbors,
- getting in touch with people you know in the area,
- calling or writing the chamber of commerce for information,
- studying maps and booklets about the area, and
- looking through the Yellow Pages (in the phone book).

Step Four: Decide what you can do about it.

Determine what you can do to make the move a positive experience for yourself and the people around you.

You might decide to do these things before you move:

- Before you say good-bye, get the addresses and telephone numbers of your special friends and neighbors so you can keep in touch with them.
- Collect photographs and mementos from the community you will be leaving. Store these items in a scrapbook or special box.
- Help your family pack. Ask your parents to let you pack your own belongings.
- Make an effort to be kind to other members of your family and remember that moving can be hard on everyone.

You might decide to do these things to help yourself feel better after you move to your new home:

- Unpack your own belongings and set up your own bedroom.
- Make new friends and get involved in your community as soon as possible.
- Concentrate on finding things you like about the new community.
- Telephone or write letters to your special friends and neighbors from the community where you used to live.
- Look over your photographs and mementos from the community you left.
- Talk to your family about how you are feeling about the move.

Step Five: Follow through with your decisions.

Do the things you have decided to do. This will give you a sense of control over the move.

Step Six: Continue to talk about the change until you have adapted to it.

Talking about a change makes it easier to adapt to it. Make sure that you share your thoughts and feelings with a person who is understanding enough to respect and honor them.

It will be easier for you to adapt to a move if you avoid doing these things:

Avoid pretending that moving does *not* bother you if it actually does.

Avoid saying or doing unpleasant things in an effort to stop the move from happening.

Avoid saying or doing things to make the people around you feel bad about moving.

Avoid trying to forget the people, places, and things that you are leaving behind in an effort to keep from missing them.

Moving can be an unwanted change. However, if you handle it appropriately, you can adapt to it and make it a positive experience rather than a negative one.

This is true of all the unwanted changes that you might encounter.

It is important to remember this:

The changes you experience, whether they are wanted or unwanted, are a part of living. They make it possible for you to grow and live a healthy, productive life.